Other Giftbooks by Exley

Happiness Quotations   Wishing you Happiness

Garden Lover's Quotations   Flowers a Celebration

Published simultaneously in 1996 by Exley Publications in Great Britain, and Exley Giftbooks in the USA.

Copyright © Helen Exley 1996

12 11 10 9 8 7 6

ISBN 1-85015-646-8

Edited and pictures selected by Helen Exley.
Picture research by Image Select International.
Typeset by Delta, Watford.
Printed in Hungary.

Exley Publications Ltd., 16 Chalk Hill, Watford, Herts WD1 4BN, UK.
Exley Publications LLC, 232 Madison Avenue, Suite 1206, NY 10016, USA.

Acknowledgements: The publishers are grateful for permission to reproduce copyright material. While every effort has been made to trace copyright holders, the publishers would be pleased to hear from any not here acknowledged. THICH NHAT HANH: Reprinted from *"Being Peace"*, with permission of Parallax Press 1987, Berkeley, California. J. DONALD WALTERS: Author of *"Superconsciousness, A Guide to Meditation"*, extract from *"Secrets of Happiness"*, © Crystal Clarity Publishers 1993, Nevada City, California. HENRY VAN DYKE: Reprinted by permission of Macmillan General Reference Publishing, New York. NAOMI SHIHAB NYE: "So Much Happiness" extract from *"Hugging the Jukebox"* © Naomi Shihab Nye.

Picture Credits: Archiv für Kunst (AKG), Bridgeman Art Library (BAL), Fine Art Photographic (FAP), Scala (SCA), Statens Konstmuseer, Stockholm, (SK). Cover: Pal Szintei Merse, The Poppy Field, BAL; title page: © 1995 Patrick William Adam, Morning in the Studio, FAP; p.7: © 1995 Lillian Delevoryas, Nasturtiums in a blue vase, BAL; p.8: © 1995 Eugene Montezin, Garden in Bloom, AKG; p.10: Kowalski-Wierusz, AKG; p.12: © 1995 Lucy Willis, Chris Beetles Gallery; p.14: Pierre Auguste Renoir, SCA; p.17: Jules Ferdinand Medard, FAP; p.18: Carl Larsson, SK; p.20: © 1995 Henri-Gaston Darien, FAP; p.22: © 1995 Linda Benton, Daisies and Phlox, BAL; p.25: © 1995 Kevin Macpherson, Wild red poppies, Image Bank; p.26: © 1995 William Edward Lewis Bunn, Festival at Hamburg, NMAA/SAPA; p.29: Canegallo, Alinari; p.31: Maurice Prendergast, Art Resource; p.32: © 1995 Linda Benton, Poppies and Irises, BAL; p.35: © 1995 David Gould, Head of a Girl, BAL; p.36: Young Woman, AKG; p.38: © 1995 Linda Benton, Poppies, BAL; p.41: © 1995 Kevin Macpherson, Rose Garden, Image Bank; p.43: Adolph von Menzel, AKG; p.44: Vito D'Ancona, SCA; p.47: Vincent van Gogh, AKG; p.48: © 1995 Diana Armfield, BAL; p.50: Maurice Prendergast, New England 1912, BAL; p.53: Edgar Degas, SK; p.54: Peter Severin Kroyer, BAL; p.57: as cover; p.58: © Fritz Freitag, Frohlicher Winter, AKG; p.60: I. Alphonse, Edimedia.

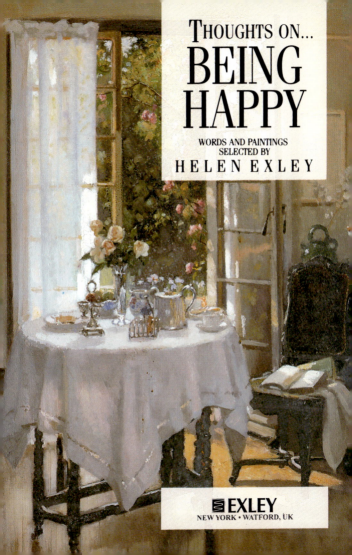

Thoughts on...
BEING HAPPY

WORDS AND PAINTINGS
SELECTED BY

H E L E N   E X L E Y

EXLEY
NEW YORK • WATFORD, UK

My joy is like spring, so warm it makes flowers bloom in my hands.

THICH NHAT HANH

I have felt to soar in freedom and in the fullness of power, joy, volition.

WALT WHITMAN (1819-1891)

There are two ways to live your life. One is as though nothing is a miracle. The other is as though everything is a miracle.

ALBERT EINSTEIN (1879-1955)

If we had keen vision and feeling of all ordinary life, it would be like hearing the grass grow and the squirrel's heart beat, and we should die of that roar which lies on the other side of silence.

GEORGE ELIOT (MARY ANN EVANS) (1819-1880)

O wonderful, wonderful, and most wonderful wonderful, and yet again wonderful, and after that out of all whooping!

WILLIAM SHAKESPEARE (1564-1616), FROM *"AS YOU LIKE IT"*

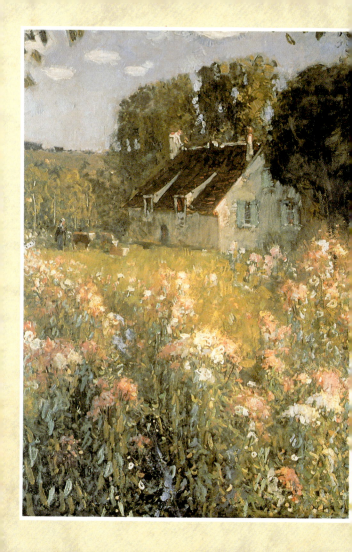

Happiness is intrinsic, it's an internal thing. When you build it into yourself, no external circumstances can take it away.

LEO F. BUSCAGLIA

Be gentle, patient, humble and courteous to all, but especially be gentle and patient with yourself. I think that many of your troubles arise from an exaggerated anxiety, a secret impatience with your own faults; and this restlessness, when once it has got possession of your mind, is the cause of numberless trifling faults, which worry you… I would have you honest in checking and correcting yourself, but at the same time patient under the consciousness of your frailty.

PERE HYACINTHE BESSON

It is not easy to find happiness in ourselves, and it is not possible to find it elsewhere.

AGNES REPPLIER (1858-1950)

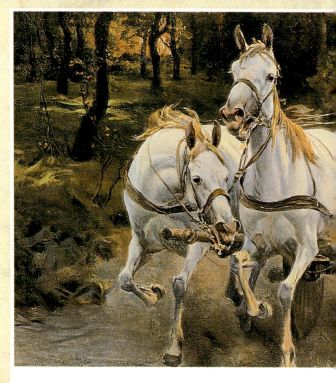

Look to this day! For it is life, the very
life of life. In its brief course lie all the
varieties and realities of your existence: the
bliss of growth, the glory of action, the
splendour of beauty.
For yesterday is already a dream, and tomorrow

is only a vision, but today, well-lived,
makes every yesterday a dream of happiness,
and every tomorrow a vision of hope.
Look well, therefore, to this day! Such is the
salutation of the dawn.

FROM THE SANSKRIT

Do we need to make a special effort to enjoy the beauty of the blue sky? Do we have to practice to be able to enjoy it? No, we just enjoy it. Each second, each minute of our lives can be like this. Wherever we are, any time, we have the capacity to enjoy the sunshine, the presence of each other, even the sensation of our breathing. We don't need to go to China to enjoy the blue sky. We don't have to travel into the future to enjoy our breathing. We can be in touch with these things right now.

THICH NHAT HANH

One of the most tragic things I know about human nature is that all of us tend to put off living. We are all dreaming of some magical rose garden over the horizon – instead of enjoying the roses that are blooming outside our windows today.

DALE CARNEGIE

The longer I live the more my mind dwells
upon the beauty and wonder of the world…
I have loved the feel of the grass under my feet,
and the sound of the running streams by
my side. The hum of the wind in the treetops
has always been good music to me, and the
face of the fields has often comforted me more
than the faces of men.

I am in love with this world… I have tilled
its soil, I have gathered its harvest, I have
waited upon its seasons, and always have I
reaped what I have sown.

I have climbed its mountains, roamed its
forests, sailed its waters, crossed its deserts, felt
the sting of its frosts, the oppression of its
heats, the drench of its rains, the fury of its
winds, and always have beauty and joy waited
upon my goings and comings.

JOHN BURROUGHS (1837-1921)

The sense of existence is the greatest happiness.

BENJAMIN DISRAELI (1804-1881)

Above the roar of city squares the starlings swirl
like smoke. In concrete canyons the kestrels raise
their young. The wasteland is ablaze with
willowherb. Beauty is all about you.

PAM BROWN, b.1928

Still there is joy that will not cease,
Calm hovering o'er the face of things,
That sweet tranquillity and peace
That morning ever brings.

JOHN CLARE (1793-1864)

My whole attitude to life is spiritual – a feeling of
identification with all nature, all mankind, all life,
the whole of the past, the whole of the future.

LORD (FENNER) BROCKWAY (1888-1988)

And could you keep your heart in wonder at the daily miracles of your life, your pain would not seem less wondrous than your joy.

KAHLIL GIBRAN (1883-1931)

Deep in the soul, below pain, below all
the distraction of life, is a silence
vast and grand – an infinite ocean of calm,
which nothing can disturb; Nature's
own exceeding peace, which "passes
understanding".

That which we seek with passionate longing, here and there, upward and outward; we find at last within ourselves.

C.M.C.
QUOTED IN R.M. BUCKE, *"COSMIC CONSCIOUSNESS"*

The miracle comes quietly into the mind that
stops an instant and is still.

QUOTED IN *"TIME FOR JOY"* BY R. FISHEL

You ask why I make my home in
    the mountain forest,

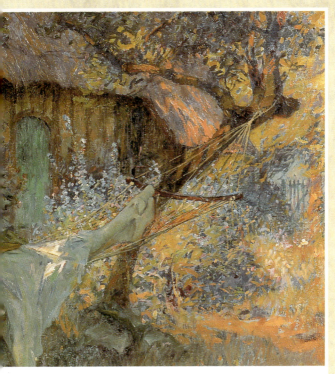

and I smile, and am silent,
and even my soul remains quiet:
it lives in the other world which no one owns.
The peach trees blossom.
The water flows.

LI PO

Flowers always make people better, happier, and more helpful; they are sunshine, food and medicine to the soul.

LUTHER BURBANK

Yes, in the poor man's garden grow
Far more than herbs or flowers –
Kind thoughts, contentment, peace of mind,
And joy for weary hours.

MARY HOWITT (1799-1888),
FROM *"THE POOR MAN'S GARDEN"*

What do we want most to dwell near to? Not to many men surely, the depot, the post-office, the bar-room, the meeting-house, the school-house, the grocery, Beacon Hill, or the Five Points, where men most congregate, but to the perennial source of our life, whence in all our experience we have found that to issue…

HENRY DAVID THOREAU (1817-1862)

When the green woods laugh, with the voice of joy,
And the dimpling stream runs laughing by,
When the air does laugh with our merry wit,
And the green hill laughs with the noise of it.

When the meadows laugh with lively green
And the grasshopper laughs in the merry scene,
When Mary and Susan and Emily,
With their sweet round mouths sing Ha, Ha, He.

When the painted birds laugh in the shade
Where our table with cherries and nuts is spread
Come live & be merry, and join with me,
To sing the sweet chorus of Ha, Ha, He.

WILLIAM BLAKE (1757-1827), "LAUGHING SONG"

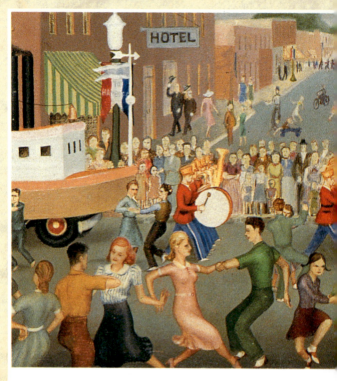

You were made for enjoyment, and the world was filled with things which you will enjoy, unless you are too proud to be pleased with them, or too grasping to care for what you can not turn to other account than mere delight.

JOHN RUSKIN (1819-1900)

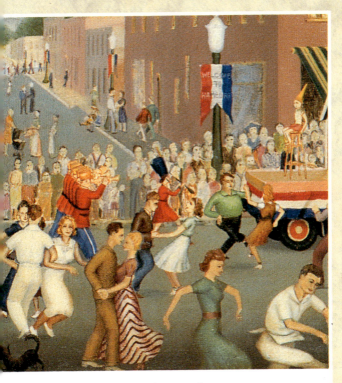

To a young heart everything is fun.

CHARLES DICKENS (1812-1870)

Frame your mind to mirth and merriment, which bars a thousand harms and lengthens life.

WILLIAM SHAKESPEARE (1564-1616)

"Henry Rackmeyer, you tell us what is important."
"A shaft of sunlight at the end of a dark
afternoon, a note in music, and the way the
back of a baby's neck smells…"
"Correct," said Stuart. "Those are the important
things."

E.B. WHITE (1899-1985)

These are the things I prize
   And hold of dearest worth:
   Light of the sapphire skies,
   Peace of the silent hills,
Shelter of forests, comfort of the grass,
Music of birds, murmur of little rills,
Shadows of cloud that swiftly pass
   And, after showers,
   The smell of flowers
   And of the good brown earth –
And best of all, along the way, friendship and
   mirth.

HENRY VAN DYKE (1852-1933)

If happiness truly consisted in physical ease and freedom from care, then the happiest individual would not be either a man or a woman; it would be, I think, an American cow.

WILLIAM LYON PHELPS

To awaken each morning with a smile brightening my face; to greet the day with reverence for the opportunities it contains; to approach my work with a clean mind; to hold ever before me, even in the doing of little things, the Ultimate Purpose toward which I am working; to meet men and women with laughter on my lips and love in my heart; to be gentle, kind, and courteous through all the hours; to approach the night with weariness that ever woos sleep and the joy that comes from work well done – this is how I desire to waste wisely my days.

THOMAS DEKKER (c.1570-c.1641)

Thank God every morning when you get up that you have something to do that day which must be done, whether you like it or not.

CHARLES KINGSLEY (1819-1875)

Riva
San Biagio
Prendergast

Sometimes our thoughts turn back toward a corner in a forest, or the end of a bank, or an orchard powdered with flowers, seen but a single time on some gay day, yet remaining in our hearts and leaving in soul and body an unappeased desire which is not to be forgotten, a feeling that

we have just rubbed elbows with happiness.

GUY DE MAUPASSANT (1850-1893)

The happiest man is he who learns from nature
the lesson of worship.

RALPH WALDO EMERSON (1803-1882)

The capacity to be alone becomes linked with self-discovery and self-realization; with becoming aware of one's deepest needs, feelings, and impulses.

ANTHONY STORR

… it is not physical solitude that actually separates one from other men, not physical isolation, but spiritual isolation. It is not the desert island nor the stony wilderness that cuts you from the people you love. It is the wilderness in the mind, the desert wastes in the heart through which one wanders lost and a stranger. When one is a stranger to oneself then one is estranged from others, too. If one is out of touch with oneself, then one cannot touch others… Only when one is connected to others… And for me, the core, the inner spring, can best be refound through silence.

ANNE MORROW LINDBERGH, b.1906

Solitude is freedom. It's an anchor, an anchor in the void. You're anchored to nothing, and that's my definition of freedom.

JOHN LILLY

You will never enjoy the world aright till the sea itself floweth in your veins, till you are clothed with the heavens and crowned with the stars.

THOMAS TRAHERNE (c.1636-1674)

If you're seeking freedom
Seek it on the mountains,
God's sunlight on your shoulders,
The wind in your hair.

J. DONALD WALTERS

One does not need to fast for days and
meditate for hours at a time to
experience the sense of sublime mystery
which constantly envelops us. All one
need do is notice intelligently, if even for
a brief moment, a blossoming tree, a
forest flooded with autumn colors, an
infant smiling.

SIMON GREENBERG

My heart leaps up when I behold
A rainbow in the sky:
So was it when my life began;
So is it now I am a man;
So be it when I shall grow old,
Or let me die!…

WILLIAM WORDSWORTH (1770-1850)

The pursuit of happiness is a most ridiculous phrase: if you pursue happiness you'll never find it.

C.P. SNOW (1905-1980)

Nearly all the best things that came to me in life have been unexpected, unplanned by me.

CARL SANDBURG (1878-1967)

The happiness of life is so nice a thing that, like the sensitive plant, it shrinks away, even upon thinking of it.

JOSEPH SPENCE (1699-1768)

Many run about after happiness like an absent-minded man hunting for his hat, while it is in his hand or on his head.

JAMES SHARP (1613-1679)

But pleasures are like poppies spread –
You seize the flow'r, its bloom is shed;
Or like the snow falls in the river
A moment white, then melts for ever.

ROBERT BURNS (1759-1796)

It is difficult to know what to do
        with so much happiness.
With sadness there is something to rub against,
a wound to tend with lotion and cloth.
When the world falls in around you, you have
pieces to pick up,
something to hold in your hands,
        like ticket stubs or change.

But happiness floats.
It doesn't need you to hold it down.
It doesn't need anything.
Happiness lands on the roof of the
        next house, singing,
and disappears when it wants to.
You are happy either way.
Even the fact that you once lived in
        a peaceful tree house
and now live over a quarry of noise and dust
cannot make you unhappy.
Everything has a life of its own, it too could
wake up filled with possibilities
of coffee cake and ripe peaches,

and love even the floor which needs to be swept,
the soiled linens and scratched records…
Since there is no place large enough
to contain so much happiness,
you shrug, you raise your hands,

and it flows out of you
into everything you touch. You are not responsible.
You take no credit, as the night sky takes no credit
for the moon, but continues to hold it, and share it,
and in that way, be known.

NAOMI SHIHAB NYE,
FROM *"SO MUCH HAPPINESS"*

Close your eyes and you will see clearly
Cease to listen and you will hear the truth.

TAOIST POEM

Those who seek the truth by means of intellect
and learning only get further and further away
from it.
　Not till your thoughts cease all their
branching here and there, not till you
abandon all thoughts of seeking for something,
not till your mind is motionless as
wood or stone, will you be on the right
road to the Gate.

HUANG PO

One must never look for happiness: one meets
it by the way…

ISABELLE EBERHARDT (1877-1904)

If you want to be happy, be.

HENRY DAVID THOREAU (1817-1862)

Learn to be silent. Let your quiet mind listen and absorb.

PYTHAGORAS

The reality that is present to us and in us: call it Being … Silence.
And the simple fact that by being attentive, by learning to listen (or recovering the natural capacity to listen) we can find ourself engulfed in such happiness that it cannot be explained: the happiness of being at one with everything in that hidden ground of Love for which there can be no explanations…
May we all grow in grace and peace, and not neglect the silence that is printed in the centre of our being.
It will not fail us.

THOMAS MERTON (1915-1968)

Perfect bliss grows only in the heart made tranquil.

HINDU PROVERB

Have the courage to be alone…
for once try to endure your own company
for a while…
Don't speak, then, not even with yourself nor
with the others with whom we dispute
even when they are not there. Wait. Listen…
Endure yourself!

KARL RAHNER (1904-1984)

Every form of happiness is private.
Our greatest moments are personal,
self-motivated, not to be touched. The
things which are sacred or precious to
us are the things we withdraw from
promiscuous sharing.

AYN RAND (1905-1982)

Never do I close my door behind me without
being conscious that I am carrying out an act of
charity towards myself.

PETER HØEG

That the birds of worry and care fly above your head, this you cannot change. But that they build nests in your hair, this you can prevent.

CHINESE PROVERB

O joy, that seekest me through pain,
I cannot close my heart to thee;
I trace the rainbow through the rain,
And feel that promise is not vain
That morn shall tearless be.

GEORGE MATHESON

If you believe your own mistakes have destroyed happiness, accept the fact. Put it aside. You cannot go back for another try.
Learn. Move on.
You are wiser now.
You can never reshape the past – but you *can* shape the present.

PAM BROWN, b.1928

One thing I know: the only ones among you who will be really happy are those who will have sought and found how to serve.

ALBERT SCHWEITZER (1875-1965)

The happiness of life is made up of minute fractions – the little soon-forgotten charities of a kiss or a smile, a kind look, or heart-felt compliment.

SAMUEL COLERIDGE-TAYLOR (1875-1912)

Those who bring sunshine into the lives of others, cannot keep it from themselves.

SIR JAMES M. BARRIE (1860-1937)

In the pursuit of happiness half the world is on the wrong scent. They think it consists in having and getting, and in being served by others. Happiness is really found in giving and in serving others.

HENRY DRUMMOND (1851-1897)

Above all, let us never forget that an act of goodness is in itself an act of happiness.
It is the flower of a long inner life
of joy and contentment; it tells
of peaceful hours and days on the sunniest heights of our soul.

MAURICE MAETERLINCK (1862-1949)

If you have not often felt the joy of doing a kind act, you have neglected much, and most of all yourself.

A. NEILEN

Oh, the wild joys of living! the leaping
　　from rock to rock,
The strong rending of boughs from
　　the fir-tree, the cool silver shock
Of the plunge in the pool's living water,
　　the hunt of the bear,
And the sultriness showing the lion
　　is couched in his lair.
And the meal, the rich dates yellowed
　　over the gold dust divine…
And the sleep in the dried river-channel
　　where bulrushes tell
That the water was wont to go warbling
　　so softly and well.
How good is man's life, the mere living!
　　how fit to employ
All the heart and the soul and the senses
　　forever in joy!

ROBERT BROWNING (1812-1889)

The great sea
Has sent me adrift,
It moves me as the weed in a great river,
Earth and the great weather
Move me,
Have carried me away
And move my inward parts with joy.

UVAVNUK,"ESKIMO SONG"

I was set free! I dissolved in the sea, became
white sails and flying spray, became beauty
and rhythm, became moonlight and the ship
and the high dim-starred sky! I belonged,
without past or future, within peace and unity
and a wild joy, within something greater than
my own life, or the life of Man, to Life itself!

EUGENE O'NEILL (1888-1953),
FROM "LONG DAY'S JOURNEY INTO NIGHT"

He is the happiest, be he king or peasant, who
finds peace in his home.

JOHANN WOLFGANG VON GOETHE (1749-1832)

Who loves the rain,
And loves his home,
And looks on life with quiet eyes,
Him will I follow through the storm,
And at his hearth-fire keep me warm;
Nor hell nor heaven shall that soul surprise
Who loves the rain,
And loves his home,
And looks on life with quiet eyes.

FRANCES SHAW

Learn to value yourself, which means to fight for your happiness.

AYN RAND (1905-1982)

The real thing in life, is to be happy. The older I get the more convinced I am that no ambition is worth pursuing except that of being rather happier… I would not give a brass button to be the greatest general that ever won a battle or even I think the greatest statesman that ever bamboozled the world. But I should like to be quite happy to the last day of my life, and to be able to inspire affection at the age of eighty…

WILFRED SCAWEN BLUNT (1840-1922),
IN A LETTER TO GEORGE WYNDHAM

Is your cucumber bitter? Throw it away. Are there briars in your path? Turn aside. That is enough. Do not go on to say, "Why were things of this sort ever brought into the world?"

MARCUS AURELIUS (121-180)

When in doubt, make a fool of yourself.
There is a microscopically thin line between
being brilliantly creative and acting like the
most gigantic idiot on earth.
So what the hell, leap.

CYNTHIA HEIMEL,
FROM *"LOWER MANHATTAN SURVIVAL TACTICS"*

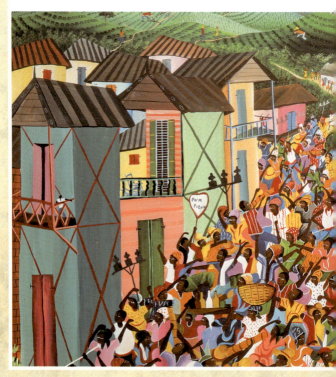

I am here to have a party, man, as best as I can while I'm on this earth. I think that's your duty too.

JANIS JOPLIN (1943-1970)

If you're not allowed to laugh in heaven, I don't want to go there.

MARTIN LUTHER (1483-1546)

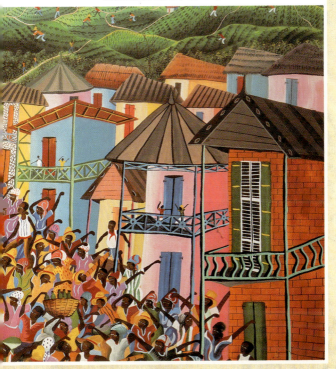